ROBERTO CLEMENTE

BASEBALL LEGEND

BY LUKE HANLON

Book design by Jake Nordby
Cover design by Jake Nordby

Photographs ©: AP Images, cover, 1, 13, 22, 30; Morris Bergman/MLB Photos/Getty Images Sport/Getty Images, 4; Bettmann/Getty Images, 6, 8, 11, 14, 16, 19, 20–21, 25; Jamie Squire/ Allsport/Getty Images Sport/Getty Images, 27; Red Line Editorial, 29

Press Box Books, an imprint of Press Room Editions.

ISBN
978-1-63494-786-2 (library bound)
978-1-63494-806-7 (paperback)
978-1-63494-845-6 (epub)
978-1-63494-826-5 (hosted ebook)

Library of Congress Control Number: 2023909011

Distributed by North Star Editions, Inc.
2297 Waters Drive
Mendota Heights, MN 55120
www.northstareditions.com

Printed in the United States of America
012024

About the Author

Luke Hanlon is a sportswriter and editor based in Minneapolis.

TABLE OF CONTENTS

1 MR. 3,000

Three Rivers Stadium in Pittsburgh erupted in applause before Roberto Clemente even stepped into the batter's box. The Pittsburgh Pirates right fielder had recorded thousands of at-bats before. But this time was different. Clemente was about to make history.

With just days left in the 1972 Major League Baseball (MLB) regular season, the Pirates hosted the New York Mets. The fans were focused on Clemente. He needed just one hit to reach 3,000 in

Roberto Clemente tips his helmet as fans cheer during a 1972 game against the New York Mets.

Clemente darts toward first base with eyes on his 3,000th hit.

his career. Only 10 players had ever reached that milestone. None of them had been Latino like Clemente.

Clemente's attempt to be the first had been difficult, though. The 38-year-old star dealt with back injuries throughout 1972. Now, thanks to

29 hits in September, he was only one away from baseball royalty.

New York's Jon Matlack was on the mound. The lefty got ahead of Clemente in the count 0–1. On the next pitch, Clemente slapped the ball into the gap in left-center field. He sped around first base and glided into second base for a double. An excited roar rang through Three Rivers Stadium as the fans applauded Clemente's achievement. While standing on second base, Clemente removed his helmet and waved to the crowd to show his appreciation.

A video board in the stadium flashed the number 3,000. MLB history had been made in Pittsburgh. At the time, the fans didn't know they had also just witnessed the last regular-season hit of Clemente's career.

2 PUERTO RICAN ROOTS

Roberto Clemente was born on August 18, 1934, in Carolina, Puerto Rico. It was clear from a young age that Roberto was a gifted athlete. When he was in high school, Roberto excelled in the high jump and the javelin. Some thought he was good enough to make the Olympics. But his true passion was baseball.

When he was 11, Roberto did chores around his town to save up for a bicycle. Once he bought one, he would ride it to San Juan to watch the local baseball

Roberto Clemente began his baseball career by playing for the Santurce Crabbers in Puerto Rico.

team, the Senators. Roberto would sit in a tree behind the right-field fence to watch the games. That's how he fell in love with the play of Monte Irvin, San Juan's right fielder. Irvin played in the Negro Leagues and later in MLB. Irvin often came to Puerto Rico in the winters to continue playing during the MLB off-season.

One day before a game, Irvin gave Roberto his bag to carry into the stadium. Roberto was able to watch the game from the stands for the first time. Irvin also gave Roberto a glove. That gesture from his idol

Monte Irvin played for MLB's New York Giants for seven seasons from 1949 to 1955.

inspired Roberto to pursue baseball. He wanted to play right field like Irvin.

Roberto started playing professionally in Puerto Rico when he was 17 years old. Multiple major league teams took an interest in Roberto. He eventually signed with the Brooklyn Dodgers when he was 18. In 1954, the Dodgers assigned Clemente to their Triple-A team in Montreal, Québec. Playing time was hard to come by for Clemente. Baseball was mostly played professionally by white men at the time. Teams didn't want that many Black or Latino players on the field.

Before the 1955 season, the Dodgers kept Clemente off their major league roster. That made him available to be drafted by another team. The Pittsburgh Pirates had the top pick in

Clemente (21) became one of the best defensive outfielders in MLB history.

the draft that year and used it on Clemente. He would soon repay Pittsburgh's faith.

3 FIVE-TOOL PLAYER

Unlike the Dodgers, the Pirates wanted to use Roberto Clemente right away. The 20-year-old made his MLB debut with the Pirates on April 17, 1955. He got a hit in his first at-bat and scored a run. Clemente continued to show promise in his first few seasons. But nagging injuries and a language barrier with his manager and teammates made the transition to MLB tough.

Everything came together for Clemente in 1960. At 25 years old, he broke out and

Clemente's bright personality quickly became respected among his teammates.

Clemente's 94 runs batted in were the most of any Pittsburgh player in 1960.

had career highs in almost every hitting statistic. Those numbers earned him his first All-Star appearance. His play also helped the Pirates win the National League (NL) pennant. The Pirates faced the 18-time champion New York Yankees in the World Series. Clemente was clutch in the series. He registered a .310 batting average and got a hit in all seven games. That included a run-scoring single in the bottom of the eighth inning in Game 7. That hit helped clinch Pittsburgh's first championship in 35 years.

The 1960 season was just the start for Clemente. By 1961, he was one of baseball's best hitters. His .351 batting average was the best in the NL. Clemente hit for both average and power at the plate. He was also among the best defensive players in the game. Clemente's speed helped him track down fly balls in the outfield. He also had a rocket of an

THE GREAT ONE

Roberto Clemente was often referred to as the perfect baseball player because of his range of skills. Some took it even further. Pittsburgh teammate Dick Groat said Clemente "was built like a Greek god." Clemente's skill and playing style earned him the nickname "The Great One."

arm. When speaking about Clemente's arm strength, legendary broadcaster Vin Scully said, "Clemente could field the ball in New York and throw out a guy in Pennsylvania." Clemente's arm helped him rack up 27 outfield assists in 1961. No one in baseball had more that year, and it earned him his first Gold Glove. That award is given to the best fielder at each position.

Clemente continued his dominance throughout the 1960s. He won the NL batting title again in 1964 and 1965. In 1966, he belted a career-high 29 home runs and recorded 119 runs batted in (RBIs). Those numbers earned him the NL Most Valuable Player (MVP) Award.

Clemente (left) poses with fellow NL superstars Willie Mays (center) and Hank Aaron (right) after the 1961 All-Star Game.

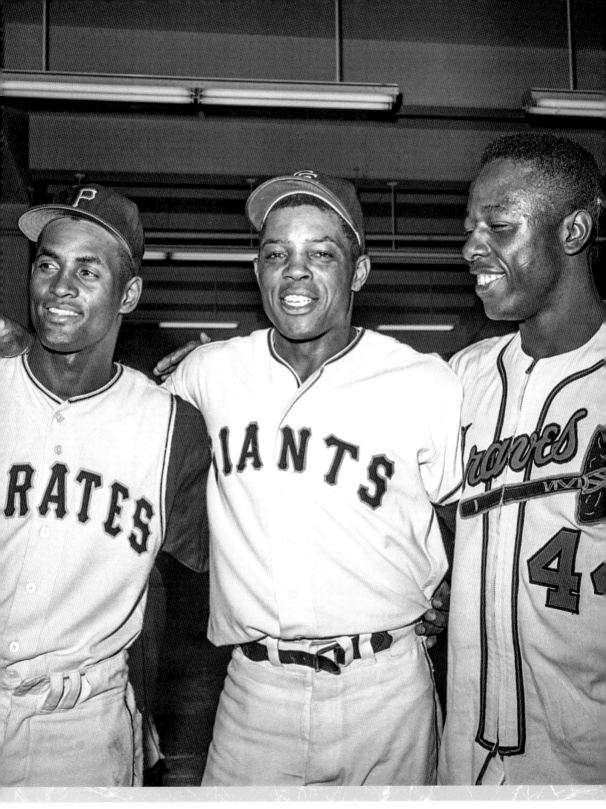

LATINO LEGEND

Roberto Clemente never forgot where he came from. Throughout his career, Clemente hosted free baseball clinics for underprivileged kids. He also used a portion of his salary to provide financial aid to people in Puerto Rico and countries throughout Latin America.

In addition to his charity work, Clemente helped pave the way for more people from Latin America to play in MLB. When Clemente debuted in 1955, only 5 percent of MLB was made up of Latino players. By 2020, more than 28 percent of the league was Latino. Clemente also made history by becoming the first Latino player to reach 3,000 hits. Since he did it, five more Latino players have reached that milestone.

Clemente's legend lives on in Puerto Rico and all over the world. In his hometown of Carolina, there are multiple stadiums and streets named after him. He also has a street named after him in Pittsburgh as well as a statue outside the Pirates' stadium. In fact, Brazilian soccer star Pelé is the only athlete to have more statues around the world than Clemente.

Clemente hosted baseball clinics throughout his career. He hoped that he could be an influence to young people, like Monte Irvin once was to him.

4 LASTING LEGACY

Roberto Clemente continued his amazing play in 1967. While he didn't win the MVP Award that year, his career-high .357 batting average earned him his fourth NL batting title. Despite Clemente's continued greatness, the Pirates couldn't make it back to the World Series. That changed in 1971.

At 37, Clemente was still at the top of his game. He was a top-tier fielder. And he was still one of the best hitters in the major leagues. Clemente led the Pirates

In 1967, MLB general managers all said Clemente was the best player in baseball.

back to the World Series, where they faced the defending champion Baltimore Orioles. The Orioles had put together a group of dominant starting pitchers and the league's best defense. That wasn't enough to stop Clemente.

The ageless right fielder was at his best on the biggest stages. Just like in 1960, the 1971 World Series went to seven games. Clemente once again got a hit in every game. He batted .414 in the series and hit two home runs. One of them was a solo shot in Game 7 to score the game's first run. The Pirates won 2-1, and Clemente earned the World Series MVP Award.

By the start of the 1972 season, Clemente had accomplished just about everything a baseball player could. One major achievement remained: becoming the first Latino player to reach 3,000 hits. Clemente achieved that feat

Clemente watches a home run soar in Game 7 of the 1971 World Series.

with three games to spare in the season. While his hitting milestone was the headline of 1972, he also won his 12th consecutive Gold Glove that year.

No one expected that to be Clemente's last MLB season. But tragedy struck in the winter of 1972. Earthquakes caused massive damage in Nicaragua. Clemente organized an effort to collect and send supplies to people there. He and four other people boarded an airplane to make sure everything got there. Unfortunately, a terrible accident occurred. The plane crashed into the Atlantic Ocean. Everyone on the plane died.

While Clemente passed away at 38, his legacy lived on. Usually, players must wait five years after their career ends to get inducted into the Baseball Hall of Fame. An exception

AN AWARD FOR KINDNESS

MLB started handing out a new award in 1971. A player who showcased great skill on the field and charity work in their community would receive the award each year. In 1973, it became known as the Roberto Clemente Award to honor him after his death.

A statue of Clemente has been displayed outside of Pittsburgh's ballpark since 1994.

was made after Clemente's death. In 1973, he became the first Latino to make the Baseball Hall of Fame.

TIMELINE

1. ## Carolina, Puerto Rico (August 18, 1934)
   Roberto Clemente is born.

2. ## Montreal, Québec (November 30, 1954)
   The Pittsburgh Pirates draft Clemente while he plays for the Brooklyn Dodgers' Triple-A team in Montreal.

3. ## Pittsburgh, Pennsylvania (April 17, 1955)
   Clemente makes his MLB debut with the Pirates.

4. ## Milwaukee, Wisconsin (September 25, 1960)
   Clemente helps the Pirates clinch their first NL pennant in 33 years with a 5–3 win over the Milwaukee Braves. The Pirates go on to win the World Series.

5. ## San Francisco, California (July 11, 1961)
   Clemente hits a walk-off home run in his first All-Star Game start, pulling off an NL comeback to win 5–4.

6. ## Baltimore, Maryland (October 17, 1971)
   Clemente wins the World Series MVP Award and lifts the Pirates to another championship, this time over the Baltimore Orioles.

7. ## Pittsburgh, Pennsylvania (September 30, 1972)
   Clemente becomes the first Latino player to reach 3,000 hits.

8. ## Cooperstown, New York (March 20, 1973)
   Clemente becomes the first Latino inducted into the Baseball Hall of Fame.

MAP

AT A GLANCE

Birth date: August 18, 1934

Birthplace: Carolina, Puerto Rico

Died: December 31, 1972

Position: Right field

Size: 5-foot-11 (180 cm), 175 pounds (79 kg)

Team: Pittsburgh Pirates (1955–72)

Major awards: NL MVP (1966), World Series champion (1960, 1971), World Series MVP (1971), NL batting title (1961, 1964–65, 1967), Gold Glove (1961–72), Baseball Hall of Fame (1973)

GLOSSARY

assists
Times when a fielder throws the ball to help another player record an out.

clutch
A player who thrives late in games or in pressure-filled situations.

idol
A person who is greatly admired.

legacy
The way a person is remembered, as well as the changes they helped to make.

Negro Leagues
Professional baseball leagues for Black players in the 1800s and 1900s when baseball was segregated.

passion
Something a person really loves or cares about.

pennant
A banner earned by the winners of the American League and National League every year.

Triple-A
The highest level of Minor League Baseball.

TO LEARN MORE

Books

Donnelly, Patrick. *Pittsburgh Pirates*. Minneapolis: Abdo Publishing, 2023.

Romo Edelman, Claudia, and Sara E. Echenique. *Hispanic Star: Roberto Clemente*. New York: Roaring Brook Press, 2022.

Starr, Abbe L. *Roberto Clemente: Baseball's Biggest Heart*. Minneapolis: Lerner Publications, 2023.

More Information

To learn more about Roberto Clemente, go to **pressboxbooks.com/AllAccess**.

These links are routinely monitored and updated to provide the most current information available.

INDEX